Piano · Vocal · Guitar

LIONEL RICHIE ◆ T   EE

LIONEL RICHIE
TUSKEGEE

ISBN 978-1-4768-1454-4

HAL•LEONARD®
CORPORATION

7777 W. BLUEMOUND RD. P.O. BOX 13819 MILWAUKEE, WI 53213

Visit Hal Leonard Online at
www.halleonard.com

YOU ARE

Words and Music by LIONEL RICHIE
and BRENDA HARVEY-RICHIE

Moderate Pop Rock

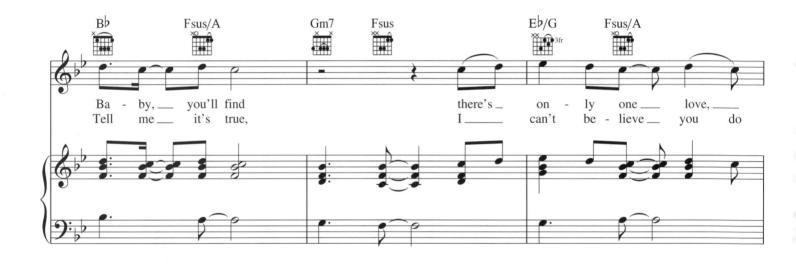

Ba - by, _ you'll find there's _ on - ly one _ love, _
Tell me _ it's true, I _ can't be - lieve _ you do

yours and mine. I've _ got so _ much _ love.
what you do. I've _ got so _ much _ love.

and I'd do it all a-gain and a-gain. _____ Oh. _____

Oh. _____ Oh. _____

I know you know the way I feel and

SAY YOU, SAY ME

Words and Music by
LIONEL RICHIE

Moderately
G
D/F♯
Em
G/D
C
Dsus
mp
G
D/F♯
Em
G/D
C
Dsus
G
G
D/F♯
Say you, say me,
Em
G/D
C
Dsus
G
say it for al - ways, that's the way it should be.

STUCK ON YOU

Words and Music by
LIONEL RICHIE

Stuck on you, _ got this feel-ing down deep in my soul _ that I just _ can't lose, _
Stuck on you, _ been a fool too long, _ I guess it's time for me to come on home, _

guess I'm on _ my _ way. _
guess I'm on _ my _ way. _

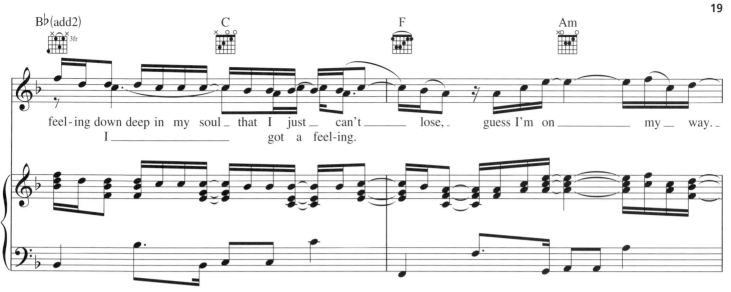

feel-ing down deep in my soul _ that I just _ can't _ lose, _ guess I'm on _ my _ way. _
I _ got a feel-ing.

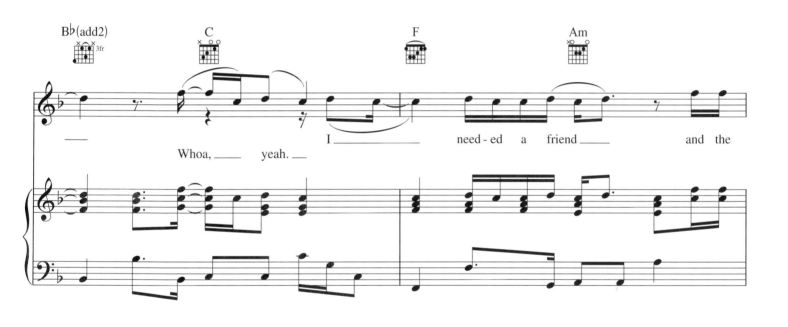

_ Whoa, _ yeah. _
I _ need-ed a friend _ and the

way I feel now, I guess I'll _ be with you _ 'til the end. _ Guess I'm on _ my _

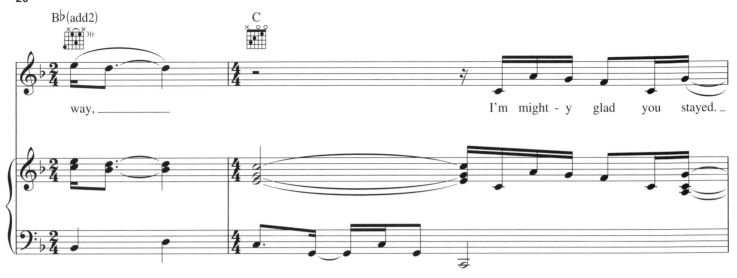

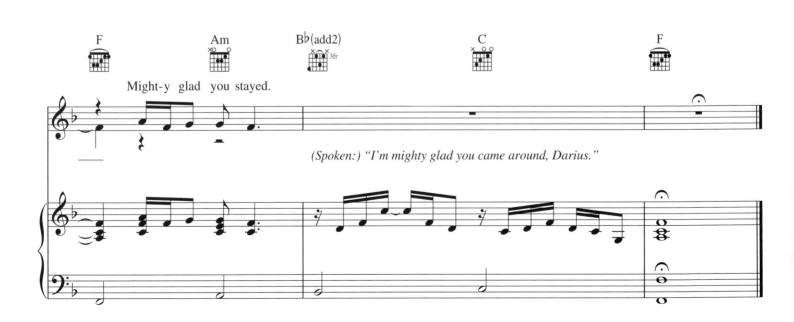

DEEP RIVER WOMAN

Words and Music by
LIONEL RICHIE

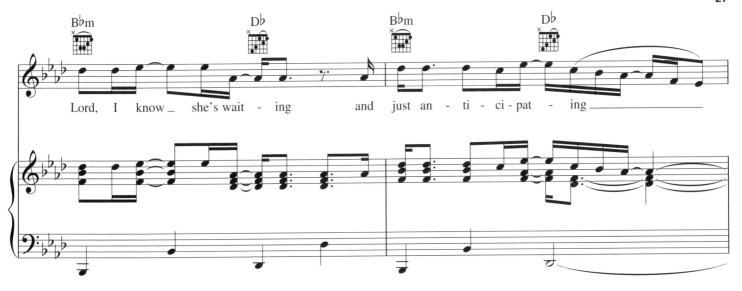

Lord, I know _ she's wait - ing and just an - ti - ci - pat - ing _

all my love. _

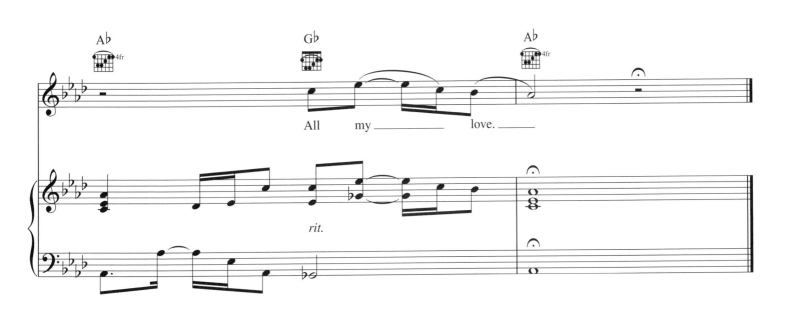

All my _ love. _

rit.

MY LOVE

Words and Music by
LIONEL RICHIE

34

Vocal ad lib. on repeats

all _____ the time. _____ All the time.

All the time. _____ My love, _

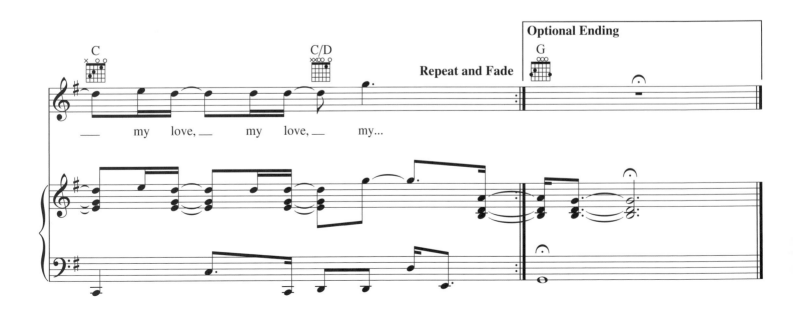

__ my love, __ my love, __ my...

Repeat and Fade

Optional Ending

DANCING ON THE CEILING

Words by LIONEL RICHIE
Music by LIONEL RICHIE,
CARLOS RIOS and MICHAEL FRENCHIK

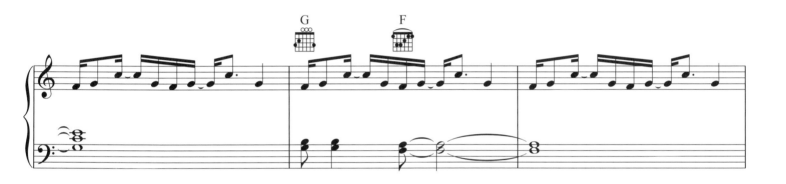

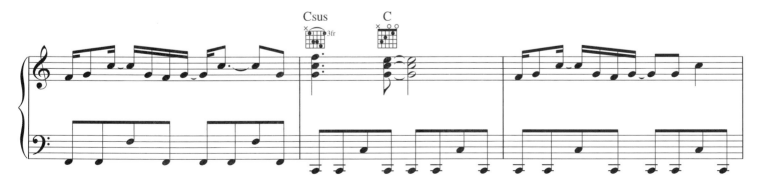

HELLO

Words and Music by
LIONEL RICHIE

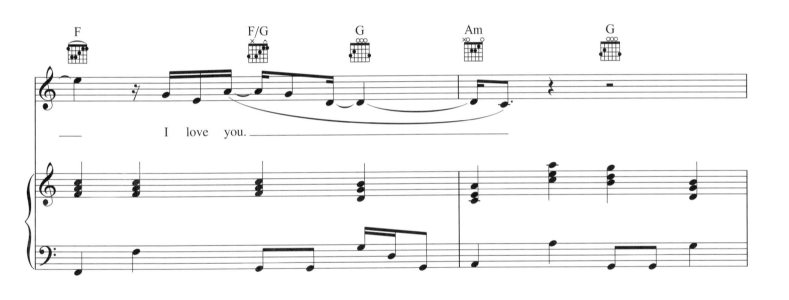

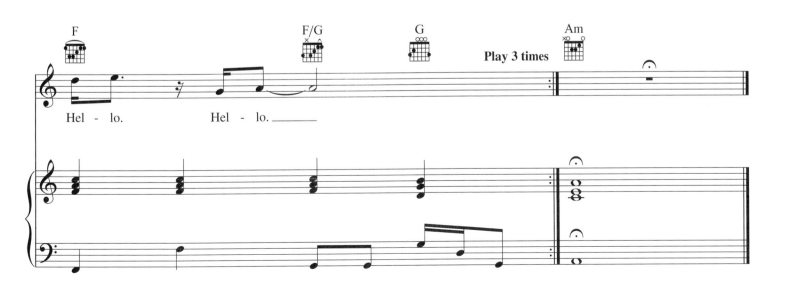

SAIL ON

Words and Music by
LIONEL RICHIE

Moderate groove

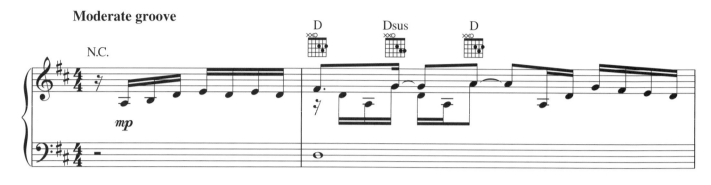

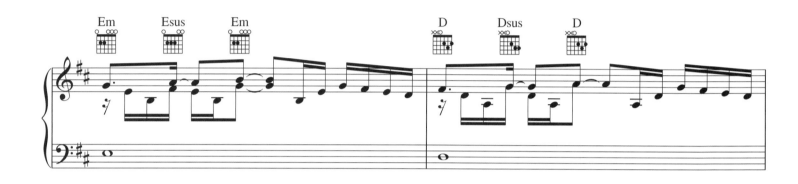

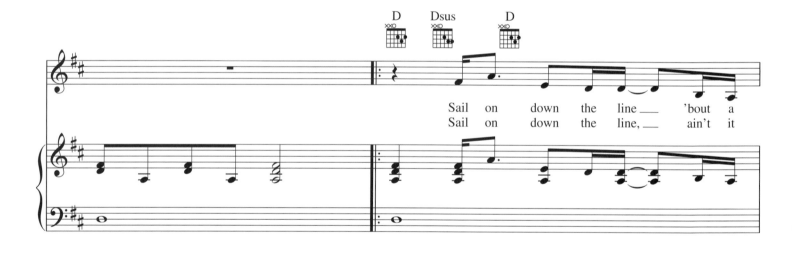

Sail on down the line ___ 'bout a
Sail on down the line, ___ ain't it

half a mile ___ or so ___ and I,   I don't real-ly want to know ___
fun-ny how the time can go. ___ All my   friends say they told me so, ___ but

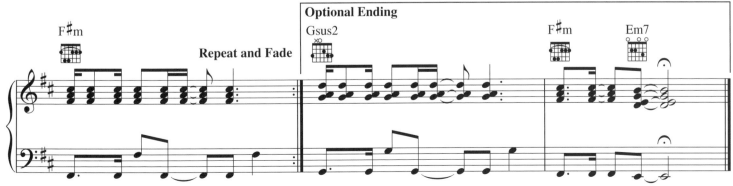

ENDLESS LOVE

Words and Music by
LIONEL RICHIE

Half-time Ballad

My love, ___ there's on-ly you ___ in my life, ___

the on-ly thing that's _ right. _

My first ___ love, you're ev-'ry breath ___ that I take, ___

JUST FOR YOU

Words and Music by LIONEL RICHIE,
MICHAEL BARRY and MARK TAYLOR

* On repeat

LADY

Words and Music by
LIONEL RICHIE

C/B♭   F   C/E

there's _____ some - thing   I _____ want ____ you _____ to

Dm   C   B♭   F/A   Gm7

You're the   love ___ of   my   life. _____

know. _____   You're the   love ___ of   my ___ life,

C7sus   Dm

you're my   la - dy. __

B♭/D   C/D   Dm

molto rit.

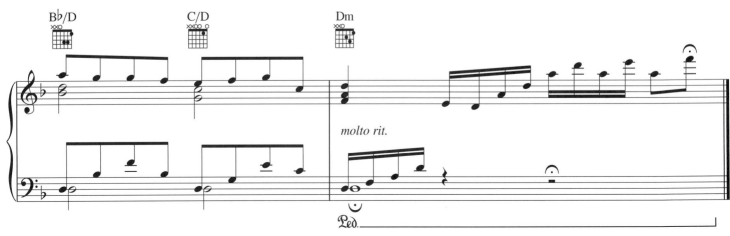

Ped. _____

EASY

Words and Music by
LIONEL RICHIE

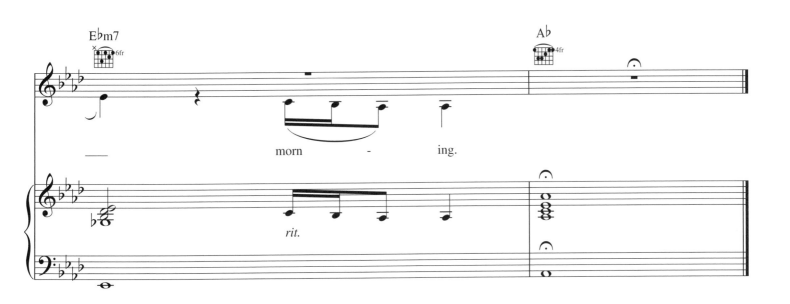

ALL NIGHT LONG
(All Night)

Words and Music by
LIONEL RICHIE